Daniel in the Lions' Den

Series editor: Rachel Cooke
Art director: Robert Walster
Consultants: Reverend Richard Adfield,
Laurie Rosenberg, The Board of Deputies of British Jews

First published in 1999 by Franklin Watts

First American edition 1999 by Franklin Watts
A Division of Grolier Publishing
90 Sherman Turnpike
Danbury, CT 06816

Visit Franklin Watts on the Internet at:
http://publishing.grolier.com

Library of Congress Cataloging-in-Publication Data
Auld, Mary.
     Daniel in the lions' den/retold by Mary Auld : illustrated by Diana
Mayo.
          p. cm.
     Includes index.
     Summary: Retells the Old Testament story of Daniel's unswerving
loyalty to God, even in a den of lions.
     ISBN 0-531-14514-X (lib. bdg.) 0-531-15385-1 (pbk.)
     1. Daniel (Biblical character)--Juvenile literature. 2. Bible
stories, English--O.T. Daniel. [1. Daniel (Biblical character)
2. Bible stories--O.T.] 1. Mayo, Diana, ill. II. Title.
BS580.D2A95 1999
224'.509505--dc21   98-25250
                                                                CIP
                                                                 AC

Text copyright © Franklin Watts 1999
Illustrations copyright © Diana Mayo 1999
Printed in Hong Kong/China

Daniel in the Lions' Den

Retold by Mary Auld
Illustrated by Diana Mayo

W
FRANKLIN WATTS
A Division of Grolier Publishing
NEW YORK • LONDON • HONG KONG • SYDNEY
DANBURY, CONNECTICUT

There was once a king named Darius who ruled the mighty Persian empire from the city of Babylon. Darius had to control his huge empire—and collect his taxes—so he appointed over a hundred officers to help him. One of these officers was Daniel.

Daniel was not a Persian; he was Jewish. He had been brought to serve in the Babylonian court when his own city, Jerusalem, was captured by the Persians. Daniel was an excellent officer and a good man. Darius saw this and decided to put Daniel in charge of all his officers.

The other officers were not happy
about this decision. They looked for
mistakes in Daniel's work. But hard as
they looked, they could find nothing
wrong: Daniel was an honest man,
loyal to the king and good at his job.

Then the plotters had an idea: "We will never find anything wrong with Daniel except that he is a Jew. He follows the laws of his God first, not the king's. Let's see if we can use this against him."

So the officers went to the king. They bowed down before him. "King Darius, live forever!" they cried.

"We, your loyal servants, believe that you must make a new law. You must decree that over the next thirty days no one should pray to any god or man other than yourself. If anyone disobeys this, they must be thrown into the den of lions.

"Proclaim this law now, mighty king, and write it down so that it cannot be changed. No law of Persia can be changed once it is signed by the king."

And Darius did as they asked.

Daniel heard all about the king's
new law. Yet he continued to do as he
had always done. Three times a day
he went home, where he prayed and
gave thanks to God in front of his
bedroom window, which faced
Jerusalem.

 10

The men who plotted against Daniel
were watching his house. They saw
him praying to God and asking Him
for help. And they went straight to
King Darius.

"Isn't it true that you have signed a law saying that anyone who prays to any god or man except you shall be thrown to the lions?" the officers asked Darius.

"I have," replied Darius, "under the laws of Persia, which cannot change."

This was the answer the plotters wanted. "Daniel the Jew has not obeyed you, King," they said. "He still prays to his God three times a day."

Darius was horrified. He did not want Daniel to die. All day, he tried to find a way to save him. But as the sun set, the officers returned: "The law of Persia says that no law you have made can be changed," they reminded the king.

Darius had no choice. He gave his orders, and Daniel was arrested and thrown into the lions' den. "May the God, whom you worship constantly, save you!" said the king to Daniel.

And a great stone was put over the mouth of the den. First Darius sealed the stone in position with his own signet ring; then his officers did the same. The king's decision was final— it could not be changed.

Darius returned to his palace. All
that night, he could not sleep. All he
could think about was Daniel.

He did not eat and he refused to
have any music played for him.
The palace was very quiet.

17

The next morning, as soon as it was light, the king was up. He quickly made his way to the lions' den.

At the entrance, Darius paused. Without hope, he called out, "Daniel, servant of the living God, has your God been able to save you from the lions?"

And to the king's amazement, Daniel's voice replied: "King, live forever!"

Still sealed in his prison, Daniel described what had happened.

"My God sent an angel during the night. The angel kept the lions' mouths shut for all that time. He did this because I have done nothing wrong in the eyes of God—and, King, I have done nothing to hurt you."

Darius was delighted that Daniel was still alive. He ordered him to be lifted out of the den. And when this was done, everyone could see that Daniel was unharmed. His faith in God had saved him.

The officers who had plotted against
Daniel were not so fortunate. For now
King Darius ordered that they should be
cast into the lions' den instead, along

 24

with their families.

And before they had even landed on the den's floor, the lions pounced on them and killed them.

King Darius gave out a new decree to all the people of his empire.

"Peace be with you all. I, King Darius, make a new law: in every part of my kingdom people must fear and worship the God of Daniel. He is the living God, who shall be forever and whose kingdom will never end. He shall rule always.

"He rescues and saves, and He can perform great miracles, both on Earth and in Heaven. He has saved Daniel from the lions."

And so Daniel was once again chief officer for Darius, and he remained happy and successful for the rest of the wise king's reign.

About This Story

Daniel in the Lions' Den is a retelling of part of the Book of Daniel, one of the books that make up the Bible. The Bible is the name given to the collection of writings that are sacred, in different forms, to the Christian and Jewish religions. The Book of Daniel is one of 39 books in the Hebrew Bible, Tenakh, or the Christian Old Testament.

Who Was Daniel?

In the 6th century BC, the Jewish kingdom of Judah came under the power of the Babylonian empire. Many of its people were taken as captives and slaves to serve in the empire's capital, Babylon. Among these captives was a young man named Daniel. Daniel was very wise, and he became an important administrator in the Babylonian court and adviser to several of its kings.

Where Was Babylon?

The map opposite shows the locations of the places mentioned in this book, including Babylon, one of the greatest cities of the ancient world. Dating from around 3000 BC, Babylon stood on the banks of the River Euphrates in modern Iraq. Babylon had been the capital of several empires, but its last flowering came under King Nebuchadnezzar II (605-562 BC), who was responsible for the conquest of Judah. He is also famous for building the Hanging Gardens of Babylon, one of the Seven Wonders of the World. After his death, Nebuchadnezzar's empire began to crumble, and Babylon came under the control of the neighboring Persian empire. It was during this period that Darius ruled in Babylon.

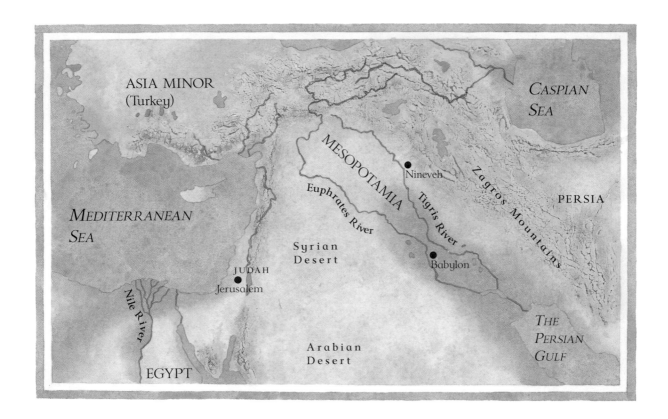

Keeping Faith

The Book of Daniel is said to have been written by Daniel himself, but it was probably written long after his death, in the 3rd century BC. By then, the Jewish people had returned from their exile in Babylon, but their kingdom was again under the control of a foreign power—this time a Greek empire, which tried to force the Jews to follow the Greek religion rather than their own. The story of Daniel's great faith and courage reminded the Jewish people of how they had endured hardship in the past and encouraged them to keep their faith now, giving them hope for the future.

Useful Words

Angel   An angel is a messenger from God.

Decree   To decree something is to order it to take place by law. A law is sometimes called a decree.

Hope   Hope is the feeling that something good is going to happen or something that you want to happen will happen.

Law   A law is a rule made by the people who control a country, such as a government or a king. The government or king has the power to punish people who disobey a law.

Loyal   To be loyal to someone means to give them your support and help at all times and to be faithful to them.

Miracle   A miracle is an event that could not take place without the help of God. The Bible is full of miracles.

Officer   An officer is someone who organizes other people to make sure that orders and laws are carried out correctly and efficiently.

Pray   When people pray, they talk to God, to worship Him, to ask Him for help, and to feel close to Him. Praying is an important part of both the Jewish and Christian religions. Some prayers are said out loud in a group. Other prayers are said on your own, quietly or in your head.

Proclaim   To proclaim something is to make an important piece of information, such as a law, known to all the people.

Signet Ring   A signet ring is a ring with a design carved on its surface unique to the person who owns it, such as their initials. The carving can be pressed into something soft, such as wax or clay, which then hardens, leaving a print of the design behind. This is called a seal. A seal shows that a person has seen and agreed to something. It is like signing your name.

Taxes Taxes are money paid by people to the rulers of the country they are in. The money is used to pay for the things the country needs, such as the police force and roads.

Worship To worship God is to praise Him and to show your love for Him. There are many ways of worshiping God, including prayers. Christians often worship God by going to services held in a church. Jews worship God at services in a synagogue or at home.

What Do You Think?

These are some questions about *Daniel in the Lions' Den* to ask yourself and to talk about with other people:

What do you think makes a good officer?

Who do you think was more loyal to Darius, Daniel or the other officers?

Why do you think the other officers chose to cause trouble for Daniel by using his religious beliefs?

Was Daniel right to disobey the law?

Why do you think Daniel's faith was so important to him?

Why do you think Darius was so upset about punishing Daniel?

How did you feel about the way Daniel's enemies were punished?

Does Daniel's story remind you of any other stories you know from the Bible?

What does this story show us about God?

4/01

CB